Lionel Messi

Unveiling the Legend: Journey of a great footballer

Carl hardy

Lionel Messi

Table of content

Lionel Messi

Introduction

The legendary football player Lionel Messi was born in Rosario, Argentina, on June 24, 1987. The arc of his career and his extraordinary journey to become one of the greatest footballers in history were significantly influenced by his familial background.

Messi was raised in a modest environment by a poor family. While his father, Jorge Messi, worked as a steelworker in a mill, his mother, Celia Cuccittini, worked part-time as a cleaner. Messi first displayed an interest in football as a child by playing in the streets of Rosario with his friends and cousins.

The assistance of his family was essential in developing his talent. Messi began developing his abilities when he was 8 years old and joined the neighborhood club Newell's Old Boys. However, a medical ailment almost caused his career to change course. Messi was identified as having a growth hormone deficit at the age of 11. His family had trouble paying for the costly procedure. Fortunately, Messi received a contract with FC Barcelona, who paid for his medical costs and moved him to Spain after being impressed by his skills.

Undoubtedly, leaving his family behind in Argentina was difficult, but Messi's extraordinary potential immediately started to emerge at Barcelona's renowned youth program, La Masia. His achievement was greatly aided by his family's constant support and subsequent relocation to Spain. They gave him emotional support as he developed as a player, assisted him in adjusting to a new culture, and helped him deal with the difficulties of being away from home.

Messi's family stayed actively involved as his career flourished. His father, Jorge, took over as his manager and was crucial in handling endorsements and contract talks. The strong ties and trust within the family were essential for coping with the enormous expectations that come with popularity. Rodrigo, Matas, and Mara Sol, Messi's parents, were also his biggest supporters during his adventure.

Messi has been able to support his family and neighborhood through the years because of his achievements. He formed the Leo Messi Foundation to enhance vulnerable children's access to healthcare and education. His dedication to having a positive influence is a reflection of the ideals that his parents instilled in him.

Messi, who had spent his entire professional career with FC Barcelona, faced a crucial turning point in 2021 as a result of the club's financial difficulties. He relocated to Paris Saint-Germain (PSG) in France despite the emotional difficulties. Messi and his family had a difficult transition, but their strength and unity helped them get through it.

The rise of Lionel Messi from a humble Rosario household to a global football phenomenon is a monument to the strength of skill, perseverance, and steadfast family support. His character has been greatly influenced by the sacrifices made by his parents, the support of his siblings, and the ideals instilled in him by his family, both on and off the field. For aspiring athletes everywhere, Messi's journey serves as an example of how family can serve as the cornerstone for success.

The early years of Lionel Messi's football career were characterized by his natural talent, tenacity, and support from his family and coaches. In the streets of his hometown, Messi began his road toward becoming one of the greatest football players in history.

Messi showed a remarkable passion for football from an early age. He was attracted to the activity and frequently played with his neighbors' cousins and friends. Early on, his family saw his unusual talent and encouraged him by putting him in the neighborhood group Newell's Old Boys at age 8.

Messi first displayed his skills when playing for Newell's Old Boys. He stands out among his contemporaries thanks to his close ball control, exceptional speed, and dribbling abilities. Messi was identified as having a growth hormone shortage, which prevented his physical development, which presented a problem for his family and the possibility that his aspirations would have been dashed. Messi's resolve held firm despite the financial burden this ailment placed on his family. Scouts from FC Barcelona were drawn to him by his extraordinary potential, and they gave him an opportunity that would forever alter his life. Messi and his family decided to leave their comfortable life in Argentina and relocate to Spain when he was 13 years old. The pivotal moment in Messi's early career occurred when he enrolled at La Masia, Barcelona's renowned youth program. Messi's abilities developed while being guided by outstanding coaches in a highly competitive environment. He rose through the ranks quickly, displaying a natural talent for the game and a tremendous capacity for field reading. Messi made his FC Barcelona first-team debut in 2004 at the age of 17. He became a noteworthy player right away because of his explosive speed, flawless ball control, and capacity for creating scoring opportunities. His alliance with other football greats Ronaldinho, Xavi, and Iniesta established the foundation of Barcelona's renowned "tiki-taka" style of play.

Awards and records abound in Messi's early career. He scored a goal for Barcelona as the team's youngest player ever, and he quickly rose to the position of importance in the team's victories. He broke multiple records throughout his career, including the most goals scored in a season and the most goals scored in a calendar year. The presence of his family never ceased to be a source of courage. His father, Jorge Messi, was crucial in overseeing his development and ensuring that his attention remained on the game. He had the emotional support he required to deal with the difficulties of being a young football prodigy away from home from his mother, Celia, and his siblings. Messi encountered physical difficulties at the beginning of his career, including injuries, but he overcame them thanks to his tenacity and work ethic. He distinguished himself as a role model for aspiring athletes all around the world because of his unrelenting pursuit of excellence on and off the field.

Childhood and the beginning of Lionel Messi's football career are examples of how skill, family support, and effort can work together. Messi's journey, from playing in the streets of Rosario to dashing on the international stage, will serve as an example for future generations. His tale exemplifies the transformational potential of unrelenting dedication to one's passion and aspirations.

Chapter 1

Messi's Journey to Barcelona, a Rising Star

FC Barcelona's discovery

A combination of luck, keen reconnaissance, and a fateful choice led FC Barcelona to uncover Lionel Messi, forever changing the course of both the team's career and that of the young Argentine. The story of how Messi was discovered and eventually accepted by Barcelona is a monument to talent scouts' sharp eyes and the crucial part they play in influencing sports history.

Messi's road to Barcelona began during his formative years in the Argentinean city of Rosario. He showed a special aptitude for football at an early age and developed his skills in the streets and neighborhood groups. His extraordinary skills first came to the attention of individuals in the football world while he was a member of Newell's Old Boys.

When Messi was around 11 years old and taking part in a neighborhood youth competition with Newell's, the pivotal moment occurred. Carles Rexach, a former Barcelona player who was now on the team's technical staff, was one of the attending scouts. Rexach approached Messi's father, Jorge Messi, with an invitation to attend Barcelona's renowned youth academy, La Masia, after being impressed by the young prodigy's talent and untapped potential.

However, this fantastic chance was in danger of being thwarted by the family's financial circumstances. Due to Lionel's identified growth hormone shortage as well as the expenditures of relocation and medical care, the Messi family was unable to pay them. Until Rexach, who had noticed Messi's talent, scrawled a contract on a napkin promising to pay for his medical expenses and secure him a place in the junior academy, the offer appeared out of reach.

This spur-of-the-moment agreement, sometimes known as "the napkin contract," was a turning point in Messi's life. It showed both Barcelona's willingness to spend on talented young players as well as Rexach's conviction in the young talent. Messi and his family bravely decided to go to Spain and join Barcelona when he was 13 years old.

Beginning a new chapter was Messi's absorption into La Masia.
His extraordinary work ethic made it possible for his skills to develop, as did Barcelona's excellent coaching and supportive environment. One of the greatest footballers in history, the raw talent that first

attracted Rexach's attention evolved into a sophisticated and remarkable player.

Messi's rise was meteoric after that time. He advanced quickly through Barcelona's youth squads and made his first-team debut at the age of just 17. He contributed significantly to Barcelona's style of play with his quickness, dribbling skills, and scoring power, helping the squad to countless domestic and international victories.

The FC Barcelona team's discovery of Lionel Messi not only altered the path of his life but also improved the sport of football. The legend of the napkin contract has come to represent the illogical ways in which talent can be discovered and developed, underscoring the crucial function of scouts and the significance of a single choice in the development of a sport. It's a tale of a chance meeting destiny, and its effects may still be felt in the football community today.

joining La Masia, the Barcelona Youth Academy

Messi's performance evolved as he rose through the levels to the Juvenile teams, and he displayed an astounding amount of maturity for his young age. He was a priceless asset to his teams because of his ability to understand the game, anticipate opponents' plays, and deliver perfect passes. Even though he was younger than the majority of his teammates, he continually stood out as a leader on the field.

The 2006 Copa del Rey encounter between Messi and Espanyol was one of the turning points in the young player's development. When Messi made his first-team debut at the age of 18, he impressed both fans and analysts with his flair, speed, and ingenuity. Messi's adventure with the senior team, where he would later experience unmatched success, began with this game.

Messi's ties to La Masia remained strong even as he made headlines with the senior team. His development in the junior system served as a springboard for his extraordinary achievements in the club. His development in the academy had a significant impact on the development of his football identity in terms of his technical abilities, tactical awareness, and dedication to perfection. The value of Barcelona's all-encompassing approach to player development is further highlighted by Messi's story. La Masia places a strong emphasis on character development, teamwork, and a grasp of the club's ideology in addition to honing players' technical abilities. Messi's development from the club's youth ranks to his status as the all-time top scorer and a global football hero serves as an example of the academy's excellence in turning out not only exceptional players but also well-rounded people.

Chapter 2

Messi's Professional Debut

Opportunities for the First Team

Lionel Messi's journey with FC Barcelona to first-team possibilities is evidence of his great talent, fortitude, and the team's dedication to developing young players. Messi's rise is a tale of tenacity and the fusion of natural talent with calculated preparation from his early days in the youth ranks to his emergence as a key player in the senior team.

Messi was a product of Barcelona's famed   youth system, La Masia, and the club's management carefully planned his route to the first squad. From a young age, it was clear that he had outstanding skills and possessed a rare combination of technical ability and football acumen. Early on, coaches began integrating him into the first-team environment because they knew he was destined for greatness.

Messi's opportunities to play for the first team came via occasional appearances in cup events and friendlies. His promise was first shown in his early appearances, which demonstrated his aptitude for navigating confined places, eluding opponents, and setting up goals. His performances in these games suggested that he was a player with far more advanced skills than his age.

Messi's journey to consistent first-team play, nevertheless, was not without its difficulties. His physical growth was a major hindrance. Messi's height of 5 feet 7 inches sparked questions about his capacity to play at the senior level, particularly in the physically demanding European football leagues. A growth hormone deficit also needed specific consideration and care. The team still had complete faith in Messi in the face of these obstacles. His mastery of the game's mechanics and tactical acumen were too valuable to be disregarded. Messi's first-team opportunities started to rise under the direction of then-manager Frank Rijkaard, although cautiously. Rijkaard understood the necessity to ease the young prodigy into the demands of professional football while maintaining his physical safety. On October 16, 2004, Messi made his official competitive debut for the first team during a league game against Espanyol. Fans anxiously anticipated the chance to see Messi's magic on the famous platform, and the anticipation leading up to this moment was intense. Despite his brief presence, his impact was felt. He made an impression on everyone with his athleticism, close ball control, and fearless approach to taking on defenders. Messi's role on the first team grew throughout the seasons. He started to play a bigger and bigger role on the team, consistently chipping in with goals and assists. His relationship with Ronaldinho, another football great at the club at the time, demonstrated the possibility for established stars and up-and-coming players to interact.

The height of Messi's first-team possibilities occurred when he established himself as one of the best footballers in the world. His on-field accomplishments included amazing goals, significant assists, and becoming the catalyst for Barcelona's triumph in both domestic and international games. With each passing season, Messi's dependability and adaptability elevated him to a crucial member of the team.

The progression of Lionel Messi from a promising young player to a mainstay of the first squad personifies FC Barcelona's dedication to nurturing indigenous talent. His career was carefully planned, protecting him from excessive pressure as he developed into a footballing genius. His first-team opportunities required a combination of timing, planning, and skill, and they laid the foundation for a career that has irrevocably changed the sport. Lionel

Messi's ascent to first-team possibilities at FC Barcelona serves as an example of how skill, development, and cautious management must coexist in harmony. Messi went from a promising young player to an international football icon thanks to the club's belief in his potential and his unwavering commitment. His story demonstrates the value of developing young talent within the framework of a football organization and emphasizes the necessity of giving up-and-coming athletes the chance to flourish on the largest stages.

FC Barcelona's First Goal by Messi

Football history will always remember Lionel Messi's first goal for FC Barcelona as the beginning of a spectacular journey that would eventually make him one of the game's greatest legends. It represents the fruition of years of perseverance and hard effort, as well as the realization of a dream that began in the streets of Rosario, Argentina. The significance of that goal goes beyond the simple act of finding the back of the net.It was May 1st, 2005, and Camp Nou was the site of a La Liga encounter between Barcelona and Albacete. Even though he was still just 17 years old, Messi had already started to solidify his place in the starting lineup by frequently entering games as a replacement to display his extraordinary talent. The excitement in the stadium on this particular day was palpable as football fans and supporters in general excitedly anticipated the chance to watch history being made.

The crucial moment came in the 88th minute with Barcelona leading the game 1-0. A few yards inside Albacete's half, on the right flank, Messi got the ball. He started a fascinating solo run, weaving past numerous opponents as if they were merely hurdles in his way, with his trademark quickness and close ball control. With the knowledge that something wonderful was about to occur, the throng stood to their feet.

Messi exuded confidence and tenacity with every move. Defenders were left in his wake as a result of his acceleration and change in direction. As he neared the penalty area, he calmly placed the ball beyond the goalkeeper, setting up wild celebrations at Camp Nou. That one instant encompassed the clamor of the audience, the ecstatic cheers of his teammates, and the achievement of a lifetime goal.

After scoring his first goal, Messi's celebration was a concoction of happiness, relief, and victory. An emotional outburst resulted from the pressure of expectations, the difficulties he had conquered, and the eagerness for achieving that initial goal. It was a moment in time that captured a young player's ascent to the top of the sport, a journey that started with a love of football and long hours of training in Rosario's streets. Messi's first goal had significance off the field as well. As he followed in the footsteps of illustrious Barcelona players who had graced the same grounds, it symbolized a passing of the torch. The accomplishment also demonstrated the club's commitment to developing young players and giving them chances to shine on the biggest stage.

In retrospect, that initial goal was only the start of a successful scoring run. Throughout his career, Messi would score hundreds of goals for Barcelona, shattering multiple records en route to becoming the team's all-time leading scorer. His ability to score goals with both delicacy and power from a variety of positions became a defining characteristic of his performance.

Beyond the statistics, Messi's first goal represented the realization of a dream held by countless aspiring athletes around the globe. It represented the idea that goals can be achieved with hard work, talent, and the correct opportunities. Messi will serve as an inspiration for future generations of football players thanks to his journey from the streets of Rosario to scoring his first goal for Barcelona.

Getting His Name Known as a Major Player

Without a doubt, Lionel Messi has cemented his status as one of the most outstanding and significant football players in history. He became well-known as a vital player thanks to his extraordinary skill, vision, and adaptability on the field. Messi continually proved his ability to have an impact on games through his goals, assists, and great playmaking from his early years at FC Barcelona through his move to Paris Saint-Germain (PSG).

Messi became Barcelona's all-time greatest scorer during his stay there and helped the team win numerous national and international championships, including multiple UEFA Champions League crowns. His capacity for scoring goals, creating chances for his teammates, and affecting the game's tempo made him an essential component of Barcelona's triumph.

Messi's close ball control, skill at dribbling, and great vision define his style of play. He has become a powerful playmaker thanks to his keen sense of timing and ability to read the play. Due to his adaptability, he was able to play in a variety of offensive positions while still being efficient in varied tactical formations.

Due to the club's financial difficulties, Messi left Barcelona in 2021 and joined PSG. He kept showcasing his extraordinary talent and value to the team despite the change in setting. His role as a vital player is further aided by his experience and leadership skills, as he mentors and uplifts his colleagues both on and off the field. Overall, Lionel Messi's development from a young football prodigy to a worldwide icon is a monument to his commitment, talent, and immeasurable contribution to the game. His capacity to become a significant player wherever he goes is a reflection of his long-lasting influence on the football world.

Lionel Messi

Chapter 3

The Messi Era: Club Football Domination

The Lionel Messi Era in club football is a tribute to the heights that human talent, tenacity, and passion can reach in the most popular sport in the world. Messi has established himself as one of the greatest players to ever step foot on the field thanks to his extraordinary abilities, unwavering work ethic, and innate love for the game.

Messi's quest to become a football icon started when he was just a small boy. He was born on June 24, 1987, in Rosario, Argentina. His extraordinary talent was noticed by FC Barcelona's scouts when he was just 13 years old due to his early display of it. With a contract from Barcelona, he was able to relocate to Spain and enroll in the club's renowned La Masia youth academy after the club saw his potential.

Messi rose quickly through Barcelona's youth system, and his progress was nothing short of amazing. He stands out among his contemporaries thanks to his athleticism, fine ball control, dribbling prowess, and natural ability to read the game. At the age of 17, he made his first-team Barcelona debut in 2004, and from that point on, he began a path that would fundamentally alter the idea of domination in club football.

Messi had an enormous effect on the team throughout his stay at Barcelona. One of the most prosperous periods in the club's history was built around his partnership with players like Xavi Hernandez and Andres Iniesta. Together, they used a form of play called "tiki-taka," which is marked by brisk, short passes and deft movement away from the ball. With this approach, Barcelona was able to control the ball, dictate the pace of the game, and demolish even the most formidable foes.

The 2008–2009 season was the peak of Messi's influence at Barcelona when the team won an unprecedented treble by winning La Liga, the Copa del Rey, and the UEFA Champions League. Messi earned the FIFA World Player of the Year title for his efforts because of his extraordinary season-long performance.

But it wasn't only about winning awards and medals for yourself. Messi had a profound overall effect on the game. His modesty, sportsmanship, and commitment to his trade served as an example to young football players all across the world. His team-setting leadership both on and off the field won him admiration from fans all over the world.

Along with his outstanding accomplishments at the club level, Messi's consistency and supremacy were demonstrated by his goal-scoring statistics. He scored goals with astonishing regularity, setting records for the most goals in a single year and rising to the position of Barcelona's all-time greatest scorer.

The chapter in Barcelona eventually came to an end, with many great stories. Due to the club's financial struggles in August 2021, Messi made the agonizing choice to leave the team he had played for for more than 20 years. He said goodbye to Barcelona with tears in his eyes, leaving behind a legacy that will always be linked to the club's identity.

Messi continued his journey with Paris Saint-Germain (PSG), where he began a brand-new voyage in Ligue 1. His influence on the field didn't diminish even when the color of his jersey changed. He kept working his magic and producing the flashes of brilliance his followers had grown to expect.

The Lionel Messi era will always be regarded as a period of unrivaled club football dominance. His legacy goes beyond stats and championships; it captures the spirit of the "beautiful game." Messi's capacity to make millions of people happy through his skill with the ball serves as a reminder of sports' most basic sort of magic.

Collaborations with Xavi and Ronaldinho

Indelible traces of Lionel Messi's partnerships with Xavi and Ronaldinho may be seen throughout football history. These alliances not only helped FC Barcelona define an age of supremacy, but they also demonstrated the unmatched coordination and inventiveness that can occur when players with such immense skill for football join together on the field.

When Messi started his professional career, the Brazilian wizard Ronaldinho was already a well-known figure across the world. Messi had the opportunity to learn from one of his generation's most talented and entertaining players during their time together at Barcelona. Messi's playing style appeared to have been profoundly influenced by Ronaldinho's captivating dribbling, daring stunts, and contagious smile, which helped him develop the artistry and elegance that have come to be associated with his name. Although they only spent a little amount of time together on the field, Ronaldinho's guidance undoubtedly influenced Messi's style of play.

But it was under Xavi Hernandez's tutelage that Messi finally developed into a footballing god. Messi's inherent brilliance was brilliantly complemented by Xavi's superior vision, unmatched passing accuracy, and tactical awareness. On the pitch, their relationship was marked by an almost telepathic connection; Xavi would deliver through balls with pinpoint accuracy as if they were being led by an invisible thread, and Messi would time his runs to take advantage of those passes. This partnership was essential to Barcelona's tiki-taka style of play, which was characterized by short, rapid passes and positional awareness.

Barcelona enjoyed a great deal of success during the Messi-Xavi combo, including multiple La Liga championships and UEFA Champions League victories. Despite frequently being used as a winger, Messi was able to succeed in a central role thanks to Xavi's ability to control the pace of a game and open up gaps for him. Their relationship went beyond the field of play; they had a close friendship and respect for one another that cut over football's divisions.

Together, Messi and Xavi made up the core of a Barcelona team that defined a generation and enjoyed unprecedented levels of success. Xavi served as the maestro, directing the team's movements, and Messi served as the virtuoso, carrying them out with an unmatched combination of speed, accuracy, and grace.

Results achieved under Pep Guardiola

The accomplishments of Lionel Messi while playing for FC Barcelona under Pep Guardiola mark a heyday in football history. Together, these two legends had a time of unheard-of success, both individually and as a team, demonstrating Messi's incomparable talent and Guardiola's technical mastery.

Messi was already thought of as one of the best players in football when Guardiola took over as the head coach of Barcelona in 2008. However, Messi developed from a promising young player into a legendary figure in world football thanks to Guardiola's inspiring leadership. Messi was able to thrive and achieve new heights thanks to the tactical framework Guardiola put in place, which led to an abundance of individual and team awards. Messi's phenomenal goal-scoring record under Guardiola was one of his most impressive accomplishments. Messi broke the previous club record with a remarkable 47 goals in all competitions during the 2009–2010 season. He was practically unbeatable due to his astounding consistency in scoring as well as his proficiency at dribbling and creating plays. Messi was able to move freely and take advantage of defensive deficiencies with devastating results because of Guardiola's style, which emphasized fluid attacking moves.

For Messi, the 2009 UEFA Champions League final will always be remembered as a turning point in his career. In a highly anticipated match between Barcelona and Manchester United, Messi's performance on the big stage was nothing short of extraordinary. He demonstrated his ability to perform under pressure by scoring the decisive second goal in a 2-0 victory. With this triumph, Barcelona won their third European championship and cemented Guardiola's reign as coach.

Messi received his first Ballon d'Or, a coveted individual prize given to the world's greatest player, during the 2010 FIFA World Cup. This honor was made possible by his extraordinary consistency and ability to have an impact on games. Messi's playing style was excellently matched by Guardiola's tactical approach, which emphasized possession-based play and deft passing. This allowed Messi to fully exhibit his dribbling prowess and football intellect.

Messi developed into a full-fledged forward in the following seasons as he showed his capacity to both set up and score goals. Messi was able to contribute not only as a goal scorer but also as a creative force thanks to Guardiola's emphasis on maintaining control of the game through ball possession. Messi and Barcelona both had increased success as a result of their adaptability.

Another crucial period in Messi's career under Guardiola was the 2011 UEFA

Champions League final, often known as the "Wembley Final." Messi's masterful display against Manchester United included a beautiful goal that displayed his dribbling prowess, close control, and cool finishing. With Messi at the center of their success, Barcelona's 3-1 victory cemented their place as one of the greatest club teams in history.

The 2011–2012 campaign served as a convincing illustration of Messi's incredible dependability and unwavering commitment to perfection. He broke Gerd Müller's long-standing record for the most goals scored in a calendar year with an astounding 73 goals in all competitions. Messi's spectacular goal-scoring exploits continued to flourish in an atmosphere that Guardiola's technical nous helped to create. Messi won the Ballon d'Or three times in a row in 2012, solidifying his position as the finest player in the world. His collaboration with Guardiola continued to produce outstanding results, with the tactic-savvy manager serving as the cornerstone for Messi's great performances.

Obtaining Honorable Titles in La Liga, the Copa del Rey, and the Champions League

Lionel Messi's success in capturing renowned championships like La Liga, the Copa del Rey, and the Champions League is evidence of his remarkable talent, commitment, and dependability as a player.

1. La Liga: Messi was essential to FC Barcelona's dominance of Spain's elite football league, La Liga. He frequently displayed his outstanding dribbling, vision, and goal-scoring skills, which helped the squad win several La Liga championships. His capacity to open up scoring chances for himself and his teammates was important in

ensuring Barcelona's standing as a major league challenger.

2. The Copa del Rey is the top domestic cup competition in Spain. The efforts Messi made in this competition were equally important. His ability to score important goals or set up his teammates made him an essential component of Barcelona's success in the tournament. His brilliance frequently shone during crucial moments.

3. The most prominent club competition in European football is the UEFA Champions League. On this platform, Messi has had a legendary impact. He has frequently put on incredible performances against some of the toughest competition in the world, aiding Barcelona in winning many Champions League championships. He has become a key character in the history of the competition thanks to a unique blend of technical ability, football acumen, and clutch performances in pivotal games.

Messi stands out not only for his brilliance but also for his capacity to improve the performance of his colleagues. With other elite players, he has forged lethal alliances that have improved Barcelona's overall performance on the field. The success of his club has been greatly influenced by his extraordinary consistency over the years, demonstrated by his high number of goals and assists.

It's important to remember that Messi's success is not just a result of his talent. His capacity to sustain an exceptionally high level of performance over a lengthy period has also been influenced by his work ethic, humility, and professionalism. He has become a full and adaptable player as a result of his dedication to continual improvement, which has helped him adjust to shifting playing strategies and styles.

Chapter 4

Messi's international career is Argentina's savior.

Argentine youth representative

The development of Lionel Messi into the legendary player he is today was greatly influenced by his experience in the youth soccer system of Argentina. A detailed account of his stint with Argentina at the youth level is provided below:

1. Early Years and Discovery: Messi was born in Rosario, Argentina, on June 24, 1987. At a young age, he began playing soccer and joined the neighborhood team Newell's Old Boys. His tremendous talent became immediately apparent, and bigger clubs like River Plate and Barcelona began to notice him.

2. At the age of 13, Messi and his family decided to move to Barcelona, Spain, where they attended the Youth Academy of Barcelona. He enrolled there in the youth academy La Masia, which was essential to his growth as a player.

3. Messi played for the U-20 team in the South American Youth Championship in 2004, which was his first time representing Argentina on an international stage. His exceptional work allowed Argentina to qualify for the FIFA U-20 World Cup.

4. Messi made his breakthrough on the international scene at the 2005 FIFA U-20 World Cup, which was hosted in the Netherlands. He wowed onlookers with his amazing vision, dribbling, and goal-scoring skills. He was relatively short, yet he was very important in helping Argentina win the competition. He won the Golden Ball trophy for being the tournament's top player thanks to his contributions.

5. Olympic Gold Medal 2008: Although not primarily a youth-level competition, Messi's representation of Argentina at the 2008 Beijing Olympics was another notable accomplishment. Messi was a crucial member of the team that won the gold medal because it was an under-23 competition with a small number of overage players permitted. This triumph served as proof of his capacity to compete on a global scale because his abilities and maturity on the field were obvious.

6. Transition to Senior Team: Messi made his senior debut for the Argentine national team in August 2005 after enjoying success in youth competitions and at the Olympics. Due to his extraordinary potential, he faced high expectations throughout his transition from young to senior level.

The fact that Lionel Messi represented Argentina at the youth level demonstrated his prodigious potential and hinted at his success in the top levels of the game in the future. His accomplishments in youth competitions and his smooth transition to the senior team cemented his place among the sport's all-time greats.

Criticism and Obstacles for the National Team

Certainly! While playing for the Argentine national team, Lionel Messi had a variety of difficulties and criticism, including:

1. Comparison to Club exploits: Messi was frequently criticized for drawing parallels between his outstanding exploits with Barcelona and those with the national team. Some detractors claimed that he failed to translate his success at the club level to the international stage.

2. Huge expectations from Argentina's supporters and the media for Messi to lead

Argentina to success in major tournaments put a tremendous amount of pressure on him. It was sometimes said that he wasn't playing to his full capacity on the world stage as a result of this pressure.

3. Leadership and Commitment: Messi's leadership skills and dedication to the national team have come under fire from detractors. His reputation among fans was harmed by the impression that he didn't show the same level of love for Argentina as he did for Barcelona.

4. Lack of Trophies: Argentina's protracted lack of success at significant international competitions prompted criticism of Messi's contribution to that achievement. He was frequently blamed for the team's failings at the World Cup and Copa America competitions for his alleged inability to provide critical performances.

5. Messi's place on the national squad occasionally came under discussion. **Tactical Adaptation**. Coaches debated the best ways to use his abilities as they battled to effortlessly incorporate his playing style into the team's tactical framework.

6. Messi was the subject of severe media scrutiny in Argentina, which included ongoing critiques of his actions, decisions, and even his personal life. The pressure he already felt occasionally increased as a result of his tight focus.

Messi's commitment, talent, and accomplishments to the Argentine national team cannot be understated, it is crucial to remember that

1. Despite the criticism, Messi broke the record for most goals scored by an Argentine player, demonstrating his ability to have a big impact on the game.

2. Messi showed perseverance and endurance by continuing to compete in competitions despite setbacks, demonstrating his dedication to serving his nation.

3. Team Player: Claims that Messi was just concerned with his success were refuted by his willingness to modify his playing style and contribute to team dynamics.

4. Messi's national team career reached its apex in 2021 when he led Argentina to victory in Copa America, quieting many of his detractors and bringing home a significant international trophy for his homeland.

Messi's pursuit of international glory and the Copa America

At the Copa America in 2021, Lionel Messi's quest for international fame came to an end with a historic victory. Messi had to deal with criticism and scrutiny throughout his remarkable career because the Argentine national team had never won a significant international competition. Messi has been trying for years to win the Copa America, the oldest international football competition in the world.

Messi's travels abroad had their highs and lows. Argentina made it to the FIFA World Cup final in 2014 and the Copa America final in 2007, but both times they were unsuccessful in winning a major international championship. Expectations were high because he was frequently compared to Cristiano Ronaldo, a player from his generation who had just helped Portugal win the UEFA European Championship in 2016.

Argentina and Messi had a sea change after the 2021 Copa America. The COVID-19 pandemic forced the tournament's postponement from its initial 2020 date. Brazil hosted it from June to July 2021. Argentina had many obstacles on the way to the championship game, but Messi's outstanding play throughout the competition was proof of his perseverance and ability to lead.

Argentina and Brazil squared off in the championship game at Rio de Janeiro's Maracan Stadium. The game was fiercely contested and competitive. Argentina won 1-0 thanks to a goal from Angel Di Maria, breaking a 28-year trophy drought in significant international competitions. Messi's tearful reaction after hoisting the

Copa America trophy demonstrated the importance of the occasion for him and his country.

Messi's first significant international championship was won, and his detractors who had questioned his prowess on the world stage were put to rest by the triumph. His outstanding performance, which included four goals and five assists, earned him the Golden Boot and Best Player trophies for the tournament.

Messi traveled a path of resiliency, tenacity, and unflinching determination in his quest for international achievement. His illustrious career gained a new chapter with the Copa America triumph, confirming his place among football's all-time greats. Messi, his colleagues, and the millions of Argentine football supporters who had cheered him on during thick and thin celebrated the victory.

Chapter 5

Records and Achievements: Messi's Legacy

Breaking Records and Setting New Standards

The "Maestro," as Lionel Messi is frequently referred called, has transcended sport to become a living legend. His development from a child prodigy in Rosario, Argentina, to a world-record-breaking superstar is evidence of his extraordinary talent, commitment, and unwavering love for the game. Football has been redefined thanks to Messi's ability to continuously smash records and create new benchmarks, and his legacy will live on forever.

Messi began showcasing his extraordinary talent on the field at a very young age. Even in his early years at Barcelona's junior academy, La Masia, his dribbling abilities, crisp passes, and exquisite vision were obvious. It was evident that Messi was destined for greatness as soon as he made his professional debut for Barcelona in 2004. His little height belied the enormous influence he would have on the football world.

Messi's extraordinary ability to set records that were previously seen as unbreakable has been one of his career's defining characteristics. One of his initial successes was breaking the record held by the famous César Rodrguez in 2012 to become Barcelona's all-time leading scorer. This was only the start of a record-breaking binge that would go on for more than ten years.

Messi's collection of Ballon d'Or titles is unmatched in the world of personal honors. He won the Ballon d'Or for the first time in 2009, and his domination continued with additional victories in the years that followed. He is a model of unmatched consistency and work ethic because he was able to sustain an exceptionally high level of performance for such a long time.

Gerd Müller's long-standing record for the most goals scored in a calendar year was one of the amazing milestones Messi broke. Messi set a new record in 2012 by scoring 91 goals, shattering the previous mark of 85. This accomplishment highlighted his skill at scoring goals as well as his exceptional ability to blend imaginative playmaking with lethal finishing.

As Messi's career developed, he demonstrated his adaptability by setting records for both his accomplishments and his contributions to the team. His collaboration with Barcelona's "MSN" trio—Messi, Luis Suárez, and Neymar—brought the team unprecedented success, including an illustrious treble in the 2014–2015 campaign. The trio redefined aggressive football with their connection and goal-scoring ability.

Due to the club's financial struggles, Messi's lengthy affiliation with Barcelona, unfortunately came to an end in 2021. Then, in an unexpected move, he joined Paris Saint-Germain (PSG), proving his adaptability to new situations and carrying on his legacy in a different league. Although unexpected, this change further strengthened his reputation as a trailblazer prepared to accept new challenges.

Messi's influence is felt off the field as well. His humanitarian activities, such as his support of healthcare and education in his hometown of Rosario, serve as a testament to his commitment to improving the lives of others. His reputation as a role model for young athletes around the world is further enhanced by his humility and sportsmanship.

Beyond mere numbers, Messi's accomplishments and standards serve as a testament to his commitment to pushing the limits of football. Messi has had an incalculable impact on the game, whether it is through his record-breaking number of hat-tricks, his innumerable assists, or his unrivaled mastery of free kicks. In addition to his technical ability, young players look up to him for his leadership both on and off the field.

FIFA World Player of the Year and many Ballon d'Or awards

The numerous Ballon d'Or and FIFA World Player awards Lionel Messi has received attest to his unmatched brilliance and enduring influence on the game of football. His dominance of these esteemed trophies has not only solidified his place among the greatest players of all time but has also changed the standards by which player brilliance is judged.

Early in his career, Messi set out on his path to being the best football player in the world. He developed his talents under the guidance of knowledgeable instructors at Barcelona's La Masia Academy, where his outstanding abilities were on display. It was clear right away that he was destined for greatness as soon as he joined the senior team. Messi's first Ballon d'Or victory in 2009 marked the start of a new era in football. He stands out among his colleagues for his hypnotic dribbles, deft passes, and unequaled ability to score goals. This victory highlighted not only Messi's brilliance but also the value of adaptability, ingenuity, and consistency on the field. Over the following few years, Messi continued to rule the Ballon d'Or. He won the prestigious accolade consistently from 2009 to 2012, demonstrating his unmatched reliability and his position as the player to beat. He was unmatched in his ability to combine playmaking skills with goal-scoring proficiency, switching between those roles with ease.

Messi's standing as a global football hero was further cemented by winning the FIFA World Player of the Year award, which later merged with the Ballon d'Or to form the FIFA Ballon d'Or before eventually separating once again. His triumphs in this division paralleled his Ballon d'Or achievements, with four straight trophies from 2009 to 2012.

Messi's ability to win these honors time and time again was not only a matter of luck; it was also a sign of his everlasting commitment to his profession. His professionalism in football was redefined by his work ethic, attention to detail, and drive to always improve. By highlighting the value of talent, vision, intelligence, and physical fitness, he raised the bar for what it meant to be a complete player.

The fact that Messi's numerous Ballon d'Or and FIFA World Player awards were collective triumphs makes them special. They also occurred during Barcelona's heyday under manager Pep Guardiola, a period in which the team amassed a ton of hardware, including UEFA Champions League and La Liga crowns. As he managed Barcelona's complex attacking plays and helped others succeed, Messi's leadership and teamwork skills were just as important as his genius.

Other excellent players are fighting for recognition, so the competition for these accolades is strong. But Messi always stood out from the competition thanks to his special combination of skills, including his dribbling, vision, propensity for goal-scoring, and ability to open up defenses. He has dismantled the conventional notion of what it means to be a forward, erasing the distinctions between roles and redefinition of the term "complete player."

Messi has recently shown that he is adaptable and willing to keep competing at the greatest level by adjusting to new difficulties, like his move to Paris

Saint-Germain (PSG). He remains a favorite for trophies and distinctions as his career progresses, which reflects his enduring influence on the sport.

Ranking of Messi Among Football Legends

Passionate discussions about Lionel Messi's standing among football luminaries have erupted among fans, analysts, and specialists for years. Messi's influence on football is unquestionable as one of the game's all-time greats, and even as his career develops, so does his legacy.

It's vital to take into account several elements that contribute to Messi's status in the annals of the game while talking about his place among football heroes. These elements comprise his skill set, accomplishments, reliability, adaptability, and the effect he has had on the game. Skill Set and Playing Style:

Lionel Messi is renowned for his superb dribbling, pinpoint ball control, flawless vision, and outstanding balance. He can easily move through confined places and elude defenders thanks to his low center of gravity. The accuracy and power of Messi's left foot are well known, and his prowess with free kicks is particularly remarkable. His distinct playing style is frequently contrasted with that of renowned Argentine star Diego Maradona.

Achievements:
The list of accomplishments for Messi is astounding. He has earned many individual honors, including seven Ballon d'Or championships, which is a record at the time (as of my most recent update in September 2021). He consistently ranks among the best goal scorers across several leagues, including the UEFA Champions League and La Liga. With an astounding 91 goals in 2012, he holds the record for the most goals scored in a single year. He has also guided

Barcelona to numerous national and international championships, including Champions League and La Liga wins.

Consistency:
Messi stands out because of his incredible longevity and consistency. He has consistently contributed goals and assists season after season while performing at a high level for well over ten years. Due to his continued success, he has cemented his status as a football great.

Versatility:
Another factor that raises Messi's stature among football greats is his adaptability on the pitch. Although he is primarily recognized as a forward, he is capable of playing a variety of offensive roles. Along with his talent for scoring goals, his ability to open doors for his teammates demonstrates his multifaceted skill set.

Influence on the Game:

Beyond his on-field accomplishments, Messi has had a significant impact. A generation of young footballers has been motivated by his success and playing style. He is an inspiration to aspiring athletes all around the world because of his commitment to the game and his humility off the field. Additionally, his rivalry with Cristiano Ronaldo has heightened the intensity of the footballing scene and created numerous debates regarding who is the best player in the history of the game.

Opinions may differ when comparing Messi to other football greats like Pelé, Diego Maradona, Johan Cruyff, and Cristiano Ronaldo. Depending on one's preferences, generational prejudices, and allegiances to a certain region, each player has made an irreplaceable contribution to the sport in their own right.

A large number of people approve that Lionel Messi is one of the best football players to ever play the game. Fans, experts, and pundits frequently disagree on his place among football's all-time greats. Messi's prominence in football is a result of several reasons, including the following:

1. Skillset and Playing Style: Messi stands out for his superb dribbling, close ball control, agility, and creativity. He is unmatched in his capacity to effortlessly maneuver through defenders and produce scoring opportunities.

2. Messi's ability to perform consistently at the highest level for more than ten years is evidence of his greatness. He constantly wins games, impacts them, and scores goals.

3. Messi has won numerous FIFA Ballon d'Or awards, which are given annually to the best player in the world. His countless individual honors attest to his extraordinary talent and impact on the game.

4. Messi has constantly kept up an amazing goal-scoring record throughout his career. He frequently ranks among the top goal scorers in various leagues and has broken multiple records for the number of goals scored in a single calendar year.

5. milestones & Milestones: Messi has set several milestones, including the record for the most goals scored in a single European club season and becoming FC Barcelona's all-time leading scorer.

6. Messi's ability to adapt to various positions and duties on the field exemplifies his versatility. He has proven his ability to have an impact on the game from several positions by excelling as a winger, forward, and playmaker.

7. In addition to individual brilliance, team accomplishments can help shape a player's legacy. Messi has contributed to FC Barcelona winning multiple national and

international championships, like the UEFA Champions League and La Liga trophies.

8. Messi's playing style has affected a generation of players who want to imitate his abilities. His influence is felt not only on the pitch but also in how other teams plan to stop him.

9. Longevity: A quality of greatness is the ability to continue performing at a high level over a lengthy period. Messi's ability to continually produce at a high level for so long has cemented his status as a football icon.

10. Global Fan Base: Messi has a sizable following of admirers who are dedicated to his career and admire his talent on a global scale.

In the end, Messi's standing among football greats is purely arbitrary and prone to change depending on tastes, historical periods, and individual viewpoints. But there's no denying that his mix of abilities, triumphs, and impact on the game has placed him among the most admired football players in history.

Chapter 6

Playing Technique and Skills of Messi

Ball handling and dribbling

A big reason why many people consider Lionel Messi to be one of the best football players of all time is because of his remarkable ball control and dribbling abilities. He has distinguished himself as a player in the world of football thanks to his seamless ability to move in constrained spaces, confound defenders, and maintain close control of the ball. Messi's dribbling style is distinguished by a special fusion of speed, balance, close ball control, and rapid direction changes.

Messi's low center of gravity, which enables him to maintain superior balance and stability while dribbling at high speeds, is the key to his exceptional dribbling skills.

This, together with his quick acceleration, allows him to easily explode past opponents. In one-on-one scenarios, Messi's fast changes of direction are especially useful since they enable him to quickly switch the ball from one foot to the other, leaving opponents caught off guard and unable to anticipate his next move.

Messi's dribbling style combines sophisticated footwork with close control. Even when sprinting at full speed, he can hold the ball exceptionally close to his feet. He has the self-assurance to face several defenders thanks to his close ball control because he knows he can go through small spaces without losing the ball. His dribbling approach is more concerned with efficiency and efficacy than it is with step-overs and showy moves.

Messi stands out in one area, which is his dribbling vision and spatial awareness. He can make split-second decisions about when to dribble, pass, and take a shot because of his extraordinary ability to read the actions of both defenders and his teammates. He can take advantage of defensive weaknesses and open up scoring chances for himself and his teammates thanks to his on-field acumen. Messi's use of feints and body motions while dribbling is yet another impressive feature. He frequently uses subtle feints, shoulder drops, and weight shifts to fool defenders and make room for himself. His feints are not too emphasized, which makes it challenging to detect and combat them. This makes it very difficult for opponents to anticipate his next move, especially when coupled with his rapid bursts of acceleration. Messi has exceptional ball control with his initial touch. He possesses the intrinsic ability to delicately cushion a high-speed throw or a lofted ball and bring it under control right away. With such a flawless first touch, he can maintain control of the ball even while under pressure and switch from receiving it to dribbling or passing with ease.

It's crucial to know that Messi's ball control and dribbling skills were developed over years of committed practice and improvement rather than just being the consequence of innate talent. His extraordinary skills have been greatly influenced by his hard work ethic, dedication to training, and never-ending ambition to get better.

Passing ability and vision

A key component of his remarkable skill set that has made Lionel Messi one of the best football players in history is his vision and passing prowess. Even though he is well known for his goal-scoring and dribbling talent, his passing and vision have repeatedly shown his keen understanding of the game and his capacity to direct play from different locations on the field.Messi's field vision resembles that of a master chess player. He has the extraordinary ability to read the play, foresee teammates' and opponents' movements, and make split-second decisions that frequently astound onlookers and even seasoned professionals. He can see the entire field thanks to his peripheral vision, which makes it possible for him to see passing lanes that other people might miss. As a result, he is constantly able to execute precise and cutting passes that dismantle even the most compact defensive setups. Messi is a master of variation when it comes to passing. To keep possession, he can carefully chip the ball over defenders, thread a fine through-ball through confined areas, make accurate short passes, and even throw strong and accurate long deliveries. His variety of passing plays demonstrates how adaptable and versatile he is as a playmaker. No matter the circumstance,

Messi's passes are delivered with the proper weight, velocity, and timing, enabling his teammates to more easily control and take advantage of the possibilities he creates.

Messi can assist from practically any position on the pitch, which is one of his unique passing skills. He is capable of laying off short passes in tight spaces to get past tough defenses, producing defense-splitting through-balls from the midfield, and even delivering inch-perfect crosses from the wing. His ability to envision and carry out passes that appear daring to most players yet turn out to be extremely effective showcases his ingenuity. Messi's passing is the result of both his superb vision and technical ability, as well as his teamwork and comprehension of his teammates. To maximize the potential of his colleagues and forge a cohesive offensive unit, he possesses the uncommon ability to modify his passing style following their preferences and strengths. His passes aren't just about passing the ball around; they frequently create scoring situations that give his teammates good chances to score as well. Messi transcends conventional playmaking responsibilities with his vision and passing skills. He isn't constrained to a certain spot on the field, which enables him to affect the game from a variety of angles. His recent deep-lying playmaker positions in deeper midfield positions have demonstrated his ability to control the game's tempo and serve as a true conductor of his team's offensive attempts.

Record breaking Goal Scoring

Lionel Messi's record-breaking goalscoring feats are evidence of his exceptional talent, dependability, and commitment to the game of football. Messi has established himself as one of the best goal-scorers in the history of the game by shattering various records throughout his remarkable career. Messi's breaking the all-time goal-scoring mark for a single club was among the most amazing achievements he set. He broke Pelé's previous record while playing for Barcelona by tallying an incredible number of goals over more than two decades, breaking it. Season after season, he was able to consistently score goals, showcasing his incredible goal-scoring skills. Messi achieved great goal scoring accomplishments in domestic leagues as well. He has repeatedly outperformed other elite strikers in one of the world's most competitive leagues by topping the scoring charts in La Liga. His outstanding versatility as a goal scorer was demonstrated by his ability to score from numerous locations on the pitch utilizing both his left and right foot, as well as his head. In addition to his accomplishments at home, Messi also made a lasting impression on the UEFA Champions League. He has several competition records, such as the most goals scored in a season and the most goals scored for a single club. His ability to excel on the largest platform and score significant goals at important times has further cemented his legacy.

Messi's multiple hat-tricks and four-goal outings are another outstanding accomplishment in his goal-scoring career. These performances have not only shown off his ability to score frequently but also his power to control games and turn them around on his own. His ability to succeed against both home and foreign competition is demonstrated by the variety of opponents he has recorded hat-trick victories against. Messi has made important contributions to the Argentine national team in addition to his club football accomplishments. Despite early criticisms of his national team performances, Messi has continuously dissuaded his detractors by surpassing all previous goal scorers for the group. Argentina has achieved success on the international stage thanks in large part to his goals in international contests. It's crucial to remember that Messi's goal-scoring statistics reflect more than just his prolific scoring rate. They demonstrate his versatility in scoring, which includes individual efforts that highlight his dribbling abilities as well as accurate outside-the-box shoots, headers, and penalties. Defenses find it difficult to contain him because of his mobility in front of goal.

Chapter 7

The Personal Life and Charitable Work of Messi

Family of Messi: Antonella, Thiago, and Mateo

Family is very important to Lionel Messi because they give him love, support, and a feeling of stability amid his high-profile football career. His wife Antonela Roccuzzo and their sons Thiago and Mateo make up his family. Growing up in the same hometown of Rosario, Argentina, Lionel Messi, and Antonela Roccuzzo have known each other since they were young children. In 2008, they formally began dating, and over time, their union grew stronger. Even as Messi's career took off, the couple's relationship remained solid, and the world's viewers were captivated by their enduring romance. In Rosario, Argentina, in June 2017, Messi and Antonela exchanged vows in a magnificent wedding ceremony in the presence of their loved ones, friends, and professional football players. Thiago Messi, the first child of the pair, was born in November 2012. The arrival of Thiago signaled a turning point in Messi's life as he accepted parenting alongside his playing responsibilities. Thiago has spent much of his life in the spotlight as Messi's eldest kid, frequently seen cheering on his father during games and spending happy times with his family.

Messi and Antonela welcomed their second baby, Mateo Messi, in September 2015. Mateo, like his older brother, has established himself as a recognizable presence at his father's games and events. Fans have grown fond of Thiago and Mateo as a result of their amusing exchanges with Messi, which have given his public persona a more human touch.

Messi's love for his family is clear in his outward displays of affection and the importance he places on spending time with them. Messi strives to establish enduring memories with his wife and kids despite the demands of his professional football schedule, frequently posting glimpses of their home life on social media.

Messi's wife, Antonela Roccuzzo, has been a steadfast supporter throughout his professional life. She is renowned for her low-key temperament and prefers to lead a solitary existence while attending important events in Messi's life. Her close relationship with Messi, their shared past, and her reassuring presence have unquestionably been essential to his success on both a personal and professional level. Despite his international recognition and praise, Messi's family—Antonela, Thiago, and Mateo—have generally given him a sense of stability, contentment, and normalcy. Their presence emphasizes the value of equilibrium in his life and reveals the sincere, approachable side of a football hero.

The Lionel Messi Foundation and its charitable endeavors

The Lionel Messi Foundation is evidence of the football legend's steadfast dedication to philanthropy. The foundation was established in 2007 by Lionel Messi himself to use his widespread popularity and achievement to improve the lives of underprivileged youngsters. The foundation has started a variety of significant projects intending to give individuals in need access to education, healthcare, and sports.

The foundation's efforts are focused mostly on education. Messi's foundation has worked on projects to construct schools, upgrade educational facilities, and advertise educational initiatives in impoverished regions in recognition of the transformational potential of education. By doing this, they want to end the cycle of poverty and provide countless children with a better future. Another important component of the foundation's charitable initiatives is healthcare. The foundation has played a crucial role in the establishment of medical facilities, the provision of medical technology, and the funding of treatments for kids with health issues. This dedication to healthcare highlights Messi's conviction that all children should have access to high-quality healthcare, regardless of their circumstances.

Messi's road to success in football is reflected in the foundation's commitment to sports. The charity promotes physical activity and teamwork among young people by building sports facilities, hosting sporting events, and providing coaching programs. These programs not only encourage leading a healthy lifestyle but also develop critical life skills like self-control, teamwork, and perseverance.

The Lionel Messi Foundation's influence has grown over time outside of its native Argentina. The foundation has been able to have an international impact thanks to partnerships and collaborations with other organizations. The work of the foundation exemplifies Messi's conviction that he should use his position to make a positive difference in the world, whether it is by assisting with relief operations for natural disasters, helping refugees, or addressing societal concerns.

The foundation receives funds from a variety of sources, including private donations, fundraising activities, and collaborations with businesses and organizations that share its charitable philosophy. To make sure that the assistance efficiently reaches its intended users, transparent resource and financial management is essential.

Lionel Messi set a tremendous example for athletes and public figures with his commitment to the foundation's efforts. He demonstrated the responsibility that comes with success and notoriety by giving his time, resources, and influence to help underprivileged kids.

In essence, the Lionel Messi Foundation goes beyond football and serves as an example of how a sports legend can transform into a symbol of optimism and progress. The foundation's extensive charitable work not only improves the lives of disadvantaged children but also motivates people to use their power for the benefit of society.

Lionel Messi

Chapter 8

Ronaldo vs. Messi: The Endless Debate

Messi and Cristiano Ronaldo are contrasted Two of the most renowned football players in the sport's history, Lionel Messi and Cristiano Ronaldo, have careers that have been filled with innumerable accomplishments and records. While each player is a star in their own right, they differ in terms of playing styles, career paths, and personality.

Messi is renowned for his superb dribbling abilities, pinpoint ball control, and capacity to set up goals for himself and his teammates on the field. He frequently demonstrates an amazing sense of balance and agility that enables him to move through confined places and defeat defenders. His playing style, which relies on his intrinsic skills and football knowledge, is frequently described as more fluid and natural.

While Ronaldo is recognized for his exceptional athleticism, quickness, and potent shots. He is a skilled forward who has excelled in a variety of front-line positions. Ronaldo's commitment to his physical condition and work ethic have helped him live a long time and compete at a high level continuously. His playing style is frequently viewed as being more strong and direct, focused on fast runs and accurate finishing.

Both Messi and Ronaldo have accomplished several records and honors in their career paths. Messi played for FC Barcelona for the entirety of his professional career before switching to Paris Saint-Germain in 2021. He won many national and international trophies, including multiple Ballon d'Or awards, and he became a crucial element of Barcelona's identity.

Contrarily, Ronaldo has played for several elite teams, including Manchester United, Real Madrid, Juventus, and Sporting CP, and he will be making a comeback to Manchester United in 2021. He also possesses an impressive array of titles, Ballon d'Or honors, and personal records. Ronaldo's adaptability and skill set are demonstrated by his capacity to adapt to varied playing situations and consistently produce results for different leagues and clubs.

Both Messi and Ronaldo are involved in charity work off the field. Messi founded the Lionel Messi Foundation, which focuses on programs for underprivileged kids in the fields of sports, healthcare, and education. Ronaldo started programs like the CR7 Foundation, which promotes concerns for the health and welfare of children.

They have different personalities as well. When compared to Ronaldo, who oozes assurance and confidence, Messi is frequently perceived as being more quiet and modest. Their relationships with fans, the media, and their general public perception all show these characteristics.

In the end, contrasting Messi and Ronaldo goes beyond numbers and awards; it explores their influence on the sport, how they have motivated countless players throughout the years, and the contention over who is the "better" player. However, it's crucial to remember that individual preferences and viewpoints often come into play in these debates, and both players ought to be commended for their contributions to the game of football.

Different Achievements and Playing Styles

Two of the greatest footballers in history, Lionel Messi and Cristiano Ronaldo, have distinct playing styles and a long list of accomplishments to back them up.

Playing styles

1. Leonardo Messi:
Messi is recognized for his superb ball handling and dribbling abilities. He can move through confined spaces and past opponents with ease thanks to his low center of gravity and fast changes in direction.
- He has exceptional playmaking and passing vision, frequently setting up goals

for his teammates with accurate through balls and assists.

Messi can consistently score thanks to his versatility in scoring positions and shooting angles, as well as his balance and agility.

2. Cristiano Ronaldo (Cruz):
- Ronaldo is renowned for his exceptional strength, speed, and athleticism. He can outpace opponents in foot races thanks to his explosive pace, which makes him a deadly threat on counterattacks.
- He has outstanding aerial skills and is noted for his strong headers and ability to score from set pieces.

Ronaldo is a skilled long-range shooter with tremendous power, and he frequently surprises goalkeepers with his ability to score from a distance.

Achievements:
Leonardo Messi:
- Numerous Ballon d'Or awards designating him as the finest player in the world.

- Multiple La Liga championships, Copa del Rey triumphs, and UEFA Champions League medals with FC Barcelona.
- Seasons with season-high goal totals, including breaking the mark for the most goals in a year.
- Many personal records, including the most goals scored in a calendar year and the most goals scored in a European club season.
- Making a smooth transition from Barcelona to Paris Saint-Germain and remaining a crucial member of his club.

Cristiano Ronaldo (Cruz):
- He has won multiple Ballon d'Or, making him one of the best players in the world.
- Manchester United's Premier League and FA Cup victories.
- A long history of achievement with Real Madrid, highlighted by multiple La Liga championships and UEFA Champions League wins.
- Juventus' Serie A accomplishments.

- Setting new scoring records and surpassing previous records for various clubs and national teams.
- A comeback to Manchester United, where he made an impression on the field once more.

Though international success has been a topic of contention due to the great expectations placed upon them, both players have accomplished incredible things with their respective national teams. It's vital to remember that their accomplishments go beyond numbers since they have had an incalculable impact on sports and inspired athletes and spectators all across the world.

chapter 9

Future Prospects and Messi's Influence on Football

Impact of Messi on Football Culture

One of the best football players in history, according to many, is Lionel Messi. His influence on football culture has been profound and extensive. He has the following major influences:

1. Messi has reinvented attacking play with his excellent dribbling, pinpoint ball control, and ability to maneuver through confined spaces. His emphasis on elegance, originality, and intellect during play encourages numerous young players to adopt his strategies.

2. Records and accomplishments: Messi has broken several records, including the most goals in a single year and the most Ballon d'Ors earned. His unwavering success on the field has raised the bar for personal achievement and inspired other athletes to reach new heights.

3. Messi has a huge global fan base that extends far beyond the clubs where he plays. Beyond club allegiances, he has a sizable global fan base. The globalization of football is facilitated by the fact that his jerseys are among the best-selling in the world and that enormous foreign crowds attend his games.

4. Rivalry with Cristiano Ronaldo: Soccer fans are captivated by the rivalry between Messi and Ronaldo. The competition has increased as a result of their on-field confrontations, and both players are now motivated to continue performing at a high level.

5. Influence on Young Players: Messi's rise from a promising young player in Argentina to a world-renowned footballer serves as an example for aspiring players everywhere. His achievement serves as a testament to the value of commitment, effort, and tenacity.

6. Messi's special skill set has prompted tactical improvements in how teams play. His skills have served as the foundation for management tactics that have shaped team compositions and game plans.

7. Positioning on the field has shifted as a result of Messi's transition from a traditional winger to a "false 9" position. Teams began experimenting with adaptable offensive formations that muddle conventional positional lines as a result of this trend.

8. Youth Development: Because of Messi's success, teams that are looking for the next

great player have boosted their spending on youth academies and scouting networks. The development of future players who can duplicate his influence is now a club priority.

9. Social media and branding: Messi's online presence has given supporters a chance to get to know him better. His involvement has raised the bar for athlete-brand collaboration and endorsement agreements.

10. Messi's humanitarian work, which includes donations to children's hospitals and nonprofit organizations, exemplifies the beneficial impact football players can have off the field. Others have been motivated by his generosity to use their platforms for social good.

Afterward, FC Barcelona

Lionel Messi spent most of his professional career with FC Barcelona, therefore the club's dissolution in August 2021 represented a crucial turning point in his life. An overview of his journey since leaving Barcelona is shown below:

1. Paris Saint-Germain (PSG): Messi signed a contract with Paris Saint-Germain (PSG) in August 2021 after leaving Barcelona. With the addition of Neymar and Kylian Mbappé to his star-studded attack at PSG, Messi's transfer sparked a tremendous amount of enthusiasm in the football world.

2. *Continued Success* At PSG, Messi showed off his remarkable talent and helped the team win national and international championships. His accomplishments upheld his standing as one of the world's top players.

3. Messi adapted to a new squad, league, and tactical scheme at PSG while keeping his playing style as brilliant as ever. His capacity for smooth integration into various settings further demonstrated his football IQ.

4. Messi contributed to PSG winning the Ligue 1 championship in his first season at the club, giving him two league titles in his storied career.

5. One of Messi's objectives at PSG was to assist the squad in winning the UEFA Champions League, a competition he had

won numerous times with Barcelona. His presence increased PSG's desire to win the elite club competition in Europe.

6. Beyond the playing field, Messi's transfer to PSG had a big economic impact. Sales of his jerseys and his entire brand value kept rising, which benefited the team and his endorsements.

7. Personal Achievements: Messi continued to receive individual accolades and trophies while representing PSG, solidifying his place as one of the best athletes in the world.

8. In addition to his success in his club career, Messi also made significant progress with the Argentine national team during this time. His first major international championship, the 2021 Copa America, which he helped Argentina win, cemented his reputation as one of the all-time greats for both club and nation.

9. Following his transfer to PSG, Messi's dedication to charity causes remained unwavering. Off the field, his charitable work kept having a good effect.

10. Future Uncertainty: Messi's plans after his stint at PSG are yet unknown. His path after PSG will probably rely on his goals for

his playing career, potential transfers, and personal preferences.

Potential Coaching or Ambassadorial Positions for Messi

Although Lionel Messi's future career path is uncertain after his playing days are over, there are several coaching and ambassadorial positions he might want to think about:

1. Messi might shift into teaching given his in-depth knowledge of the game and his experience playing at the highest level. He might decide to coach young athletes, aiding in the development of the following generation of players, or he might want to coach at the professional level, imparting his wisdom to players as they compete.

2. Messi's tight relationship with FC Barcelona may qualify him for a position as

105

the club's ambassador. This would entail advancing the club's principles, taking part in activities, and continuing to interact with fans even when his playing career is over.

3. Messi has a significant influence on the Argentine national team. **National Team Involvement**. He might decide to coach or mentor the national team, assisting in educating and motivating Argentine athletes in the future.

4. Messi's experience and influence may be useful in football administration positions, where he might influence choices that will affect the direction of the sport. Roles in governing bodies for football or other football-related organizations may be involved.

5. Messi's perspectives and observations would be highly valued in the world of football media. He could work as a pundit or analyst, providing commentary on games

and player analysis to fans to share his knowledge.

6. Due to his widespread popularity and reputation, Messi is a top candidate for brand ambassador positions. He might stand in for football-related companies or even broaden his influence into different sectors of the economy.

7. Youth Development: In addition to coaching, Messi may decide to support projects that foster young athletes' learning and development through supporting academies, camps, and mentorship programs.

8. Using his platform to spread awareness and effect change on social, environmental, or humanitarian issues, Messi might take on a more official advocacy role, building on his current charitable activities.

9. Messi might create his football academy with a focus on player development, good sportsmanship, and all-around education. This would enable him to teach the following generation his football philosophies.

10. Messi is an obvious choice to serve as the sport's ambassador because he is among the all-time greats in the game of football. He might endeavor to promote football internationally, boosting interest in the sport and participation.

Messi's post-playing career path will ultimately be determined by his interests, personal objectives, and the possibilities that present themselves. No matter what duties he takes on, his impact will continue to affect the landscape of football due to his ongoing influence on the game.

Lionel Messi

Conclusion

Lionel Messi's tale extends far beyond the confines of sport and into the realms of inspiration and human achievement. Messi's journey has won the hearts and minds of millions of people all over the world. It began with his modest origins in Rosario, Argentina, and continued through the glittering heights of his record-breaking career.

Through these pages, we have seen how a football prodigy has developed into a true master of the game. He reached the pinnacle of the sport thanks to a combination of natural talent, an uncompromising work ethic, and an unyielding drive. In addition to cementing his place among football's all-time greats, his innumerable goals, daring dribbles, and brilliant moments have also changed the parameters of what is possible on the field.

The real meaning of Messi's story, though, goes beyond the numbers and awards. His ability to arouse passion and create dreams in both young athletes and supporters spans generations. His influence transcends the world of football, and his charitable work reveals a deep sense of duty and a desire to improve the world.

This book serves as a reminder when we consider Messi's legacy: it is about a character that refuses to be constrained by circumstances, not just football prowess. It's about accepting difficulties, overcoming failures, and succeeding despite all odds. It tells the story of a voyage that forever changed both the beautiful game and the hearts of those who had the opportunity to experience it.

The narrative of Lionel Messi is still being written, both on and off the field. His influence will endure when he begins new chapters in his life, whether as a coach, an ambassador, or in positions that are yet to be determined. He will serve as a source of motivation and hope for upcoming generations. This book serves as an homage to his exceptional life, an ode to his commitment, and a reminder that legends are made via a combination of passion, talent, and an unwavering love for the game. Legends are not just born.

Printed in Great Britain
by Amazon

32055384R00066